*The Life of St. Benedict*

# The Life
## of
# Saint Benedict

*Father of Western Monasticism*

F.A. Forbes

STABAT MATER PRESS

*The Life of St. Benedict: Father of Western Monasticism*, by F.A. Forbes, has been republished by © Stabat Mater Press 2025

PUBLISHED BY STABAT MATER PRESS

STABATMATERPRESS.COM

Cover art and interior typesetting by Stabat Mater Press. All artwork not cited is in the public domain.

ISBN (Paperback): 979-8-9997560-7-7

# CONTENTS

# CHAPTER I
# ROME IN THE FIFTH CENTURY

The great Roman Empire was in its death-throes. Two thousand years had gone to its building; country after country and people after people had bowed before its power and acknowledged its sway. "Eternal Rome" had become the watchword of its citizens, for it seemed to them as if the ancient civilization must endure for ever. Had pagan Rome not proved a thousand times that her strength was invincible, her might unconquerable? How should it ever be otherwise?

The answer was to come from within. She had been unfaithful to the old ideals that had made her strong. Sunk in pride and materialism, she had learnt to live for ease and pleasure alone; she had stubbornly refused the faith of Christ and relentlessly persecuted His followers; she would have none of a crucified God. For four hundred years she had striven to overcome the religion that bade men lift their hearts above the things of this world, and with each blow had only made it stronger. But when Christianity at last triumphed, under Constantine the Great, she had fallen too low to understand its message; the seeds of death were already in her heart.

"Why obtrude upon us this notion of sin?" cried the pagan world in the ears of St. Augustine. "What we care about is that wealth should increase. Kings should regard the obedience of their subjects, not their morality. There cannot be too much of large houses, rich feasts, and revelry by day and by night. Count those for true gods who have provided such gifts for the people."

A new Rome was to arise on the ruins of the old, a Rome destined to be the stronghold of the Faith that was to regenerate the world; a spiritual Empire that was to extend its bounds far beyond those of pagan Rome in its glory.

At the gates of the Roman Empire lay the barbarians, watching the progress of events and awaiting their chance of conquest. "Invincible" Rome was invincible no longer, and they knew it.

Out of the East, from harrying the Byzantine Empire, came Alaric the Goth, tall of stature, fair and ruddy of face. Successful at first, he soon met his match in Stilicho, the Vandal general of the Emperor Honorius, and retired across the Adriatic. "The Gothic nation has been subdued, never to rise again," was the proud legend on the arch erected in Rome by Honorius in memory of the event. The writing was still fresh when Alaric returned with a nation behind him. Under the very walls of Rome, where for more than six hundred years no enemy had been seen, he took his stand. Six thousand pounds of gold and thirty thousand of silver was the ransom he asked for the city, while the patricians of invincible Rome hastened to tear down the statues of their gods, and to strip their temples to satisfy his demands. The old lion had indeed lost its teeth, and the hardy Goth was not slow to take advantage of the fact. "Give us land in the North that we may settle," he asked imperiously, and on the refusal of Honorius returned in the year 408 to storm and sack the Eternal City. Yet he was not unmerciful, this valiant, barbarian leader, for he ordered his soldiers to spare all who were not in arms, to respect the churches and all who took sanctuary there, and to destroy no public buildings. But a vast host of barbarians, eager for plunder, could not always be controlled, and the sack of Rome had its horrors. Alaric might have been master of Italy if his death, at the age of thirty-five years, had not averted for a little longer the downfall of the Empire.

Of a different stamp was the next invader, Attila the Hun, King of a race of savages so hideous that they were reputed to have sprung from evil spirits. Small, swarthy, and beady-eyed, with the broad face and flat nose of the Tartar, Attila was nevertheless a man of remarkable sagacity and cunning. Defeated at Chalons in Gaul in 451, he turned his attention towards Italy, and for two years cruelly ravaged the northern provinces, penetrating as far as Pavia and Milan. The inhabitants of Venetia, flying from before the face of the terrible conqueror, founded on the coast of the Adriatic the collection of fishing villages which were later to develop into the city and republic of Venice. Valentinian the Emperor, cowering behind the walls of Rome, was awaiting with terror the onward march of Attila's army.

The conqueror was already at Mantua, and the trail of smoking ruins that lay behind him foreshadowed the fate of Rome, when the tottering Empire was saved once more, and by the Head of the Church on earth. At the Emperor's earnest prayer St. Leo the Great, surrounded by only a few of his priests, went forth to meet the savage barbarian who had made himself the terror of the civilized world. Attila, who had heaped insults on Kings and Emperors, bowed before the humble majesty of the Saint. He retired to the banks of the Danube, where within a year he died.

Twice had the menace sounded; twice had invincible Rome lain at the mercy of the barbarian; twice had the danger been averted. The death-knell of the Empire struck for the third time two years later when Gaiseric the Vandal marched on Rome. Gaiseric, who had conquered the Roman province of Africa fourteen years before, was no valiant warrior of generous instincts, but a crafty and treacherous schemer, who united with the savage nature of the barbarian the worst vices of the corrupt Roman world. Beside him Alaric was a paladin, and the savage Attila an honest man. He was, moreover, a bigoted Arian, and had relentlessly persecuted his Catholic subjects. This "vilest in soul," as he had been called, "of all the barbarian invaders of the Empire," landed in Italy in the year 455, and met with little or no opposition. The Emperor Maximus, his hands still red with the blood of his predecessor Valentinian, showed a craven cowardliness that disgusted even the Romans. Stoning him to death, they cast his body into the Tiber and helplessly awaited their fate. Gaiseric was three days' march from Rome, and no man dared to face him; no man, that is, but one. For the second time the Chief Shepherd interceded for his flock. Advancing without the walls of the city to meet the Vandal host, the Pope exacted from their leader a promise that he would neither slaughter the citizens, torture the captives, nor set fire to the town. For Gaiseric this was no small concession; but not even St. Leo could prevent the pillage and wholesale destruction wrought by the Vandal hordes. For fourteen days the sack of the city continued, and when at last Gaiseric led his army back to Africa, he carried with him 60,000 captives and the richest treasures of Rome.

The army of Rome, her glory in the days of old, was now no more. It was replaced by a collection of barbarians of many tribes and races, whose loyalty had to be bought with a heavy price, and who knew their own power. They could only be held in check by one of their own race; and, henceforward, at the side of a more or less powerless Emperor stood a barbarian "patrician" as adviser and guide. Twenty years after the sack of Rome by Gaiseric, a boy Emperor, to whom the Romans had given the mocking name of "Augustulus," sat on the imperial throne. The motley host of barbarians who composed the Roman Army demanded land in payment for their service, and were refused. There was amongst them a brave chief of the name of Odoacer, a man of noble nature. Electing him as their King, the army rose in rebellion. The boy Emperor was deposed, and Odoacer was proclaimed King of Italy.

The choice might have been worse; the Senate, powerless in the face of the difficulty, resolved to make the best of a bad business. Sending ambassadors to Zeno, Emperor of the East, they begged him to unite the Western Empire with his own, and to allow Odoacer, "a mighty man of war," to govern the Roman population as patrician. To this request Zeno was graciously pleased to agree, and the Empire of the West was virtually at an end.

For Odoacer was much more than a patrician, he was a King, and acknowledged as such by the barbarians, who were all that was left to represent the conquering legions of Rome. The authority of Zeno was but a shadow; it was Odoacer that ruled. He was a wise man, and he governed well; but in his kingdom, too, there was a seed of decay. He depended on the fidelity of an army composed of broken remnants of tribes; he was in no wise the ruler of a nation. When, thirteen years later, there came against him Theodoric, hereditary King of the Ostrogoths, young, brave, and noble, with a nation at his back, Odoacer and his army were hopelessly defeated. Theodoric was proclaimed King of Italy, and for many years ruled well and wisely; but there was no fusion between the conquerors and the conquered. The Goths were looked upon as foreigners in Italy; they were Arians as well as barbarians. What power could blend these hostile races? From whence was to come the new civilization that was to regenerate the world?

Nine years before the coming of Theodoric was born in a little town of Italy a child who was destined to be the leader of a greater army—an army whose watchword was to be Peace, and whose conquests were to be the hearts and souls of men. And to this army was confided the mission of spreading the new civilization amongst the barbarian races—a civilization that was founded on the Faith of Christ. Into all the nations of Europe it was to go forth, and amongst the races that it conquered was our own.

CHAPTER 2
# BENEDICT'S YOUTH

I n the heart of the Umbrian Apennines, quiet and secluded in the midst of its mountain solitude, lies the little city of Norcia, known to the Romans as Nursia. Here, towards the end of the fifth century, lived Euproprius and his wife Abundantia, wealthy and noble Romans, who, besides their country house at Nursia, possessed a handsome palace in Rome. They were probably the most important people in the place, and there would be general rejoicing when it became known that Abundantia had given birth to twin children, a boy and a girl.

Eupropius and his wife were Christians, and the babies, having been duly baptized by the names of Benedict and Scholastica, were brought up by their devoted nurse Cyrilla, who loved them as the apple of her eye. The nurse was an important person in a Roman household, being usually adopted into the family, and continuing to share in the joys and sorrows of her nurslings long after they had ceased to require her care.

Cyrilla was a fervent Christian, and it would seem to have been to her rather than to his parents that the little Benedict confided his childish aspirations as he grew from babyhood to boyhood amongst the mountain peaks of Umbria. Twenty miles distant, on the great Flaminian Way, lay the city of Spoleto, a busy centre of life in the Roman world, where the child may have seen and wondered at the barbarian splendour of the soldiers of Odoacer. He would have heard, too, of the wise and tolerant rule exercised by the King from his court at Ravenna, and how, though himself a Goth and an Arian, he respected the Roman laws and the Catholic faith. He would have listened with all a boy's love of adventure to the tales of Odoacer's early life, and how, as a young and penniless soldier of fortune, he had gone to ask the blessing of the holy St. Severinus, whom he found praying in a cell so low, that the tall young Goth could not stand upright in it.

"Go on your way, my son," the old man had said; "you are poor now, but you shall be rich and glorious in the time to come." And when he had attained his greatness Odoacer had remembered the Saint's words, and had sent to him saying, "Ask what boon you will, and I will grant it you." And the answer had surprised the King, who had expected a request for gold or lands.

"I know a poor exile," replied the holy man, "who is eating his heart out for love of his native land. Forgive him and let him come home."

But Eupropius and his wife were anxious about their son's education, and the time came when he must leave the breezy home of his childhood and live and study in Rome. Benedict was happier among the mountain peaks of the Apennines, where everything seemed to speak to his young soul of God. For in Rome, although it had been watered with the blood of the martyrs, the spirit of martyrdom had died out; and many of the Christians, living as they did in daily contact with the vices of paganism, had learnt to think of nothing but their own comfort and pleasure.

Benedict was nine years old when the news came to Rome that Theodoric, King of the Ostrogoths, had descended into Italy at the head of a migrating people. The army which Odoacer led to meet him was defeated on the Isonzo, and more disastrously still at Verona. This time the defeat became a rout, and the King fled to Ravenna, which he only surrendered to Theodoric after a three years' siege, perishing shortly afterwards at the hands of the Ostrogothic King, who in his turn became ruler of Italy.

He was no rough soldier of fortune, this gallant young Theodoric, whose charge in battle was "as a swollen river through the harvest-field, and as a lion through the herd." Hereditary King of the Ostrogoths, and born of the noble race of the Amals, he had been brought up as a hostage at the court of Constantinople, where he had learnt to esteem what was best in Roman civilization, whilst hating its vices. He was an Arian like most of the Goths; for Ulfilas, their apostle and Bishop, had made the mistake of studying his Christianity in Constantinople from Arian teachers, and in the best of good faith had taught heresy to his pagan converts. But Theodoric, like Odoacer, was tolerant to the Catholics, and knew how to appreciate sanctity. It was to the care of St. Epiphanius, the holy Bishop of Pavia, that he confided his mother, wife and sister after the battle of Verona; and it was again at the intercession of St. Epiphanius that he remitted an edict that fell hardly on the followers of Odoacer. He ruled well and wisely, and for thirty-seven years Italy had peace.

The boy Benedict would have heard of the horrors of the three years' siege of Ravenna; and Roman though he was, his heart may have thrilled at the tales of the valour of Theodoric. He may even have seen the King when he came to Rome, and heard how, in spite of his Arianism, he had knelt devoutly at the shrine of St. Peter. As Benedict grew into early manhood, the sins of the city lay like a weight upon his heart. Who could keep himself pure amidst such corruption, was the question he asked himself daily, and what would it profit him to have all that the world could give if the price of it was to be the loss of his own soul? His parents, it would seem, wished him to excel in his studies, to shine in that Roman society to which they belonged. The world with all its attractions was at his feet; he was free to enjoy it. His young companions had already begun to do so, flinging themselves into its shameful pleasures with all the ardour of their youthful natures. But was such a life as this to be the end of Benedict's fair ideals, his aspirations after God?

His parents would probably have had small sympathy with such thoughts. There was no one to whom he could turn but Cyrilla, and that sweet twin sister whose soul had always been like a reflection of his own. But Scholastica was a girl, and the problem was not so urgent for her as for her brother. He may not even have dared to tell her of his project, lest her tears should weaken his resolve. For he had determined to turn his back upon that brilliant and shallow Roman world, where it was so hard to live for God, and which, when all was said and done, was but "a husk of pleasure round a heart of sorrow."

To Cyrilla alone could he open his heart, and she was worthy of his trust. Yet he could not go alone, she urged, he who was so gently born and bred, who had been surrounded all his life by her tender love and care. She must go with him; she would be no hindrance to his aspirations; she would help him in all that he undertook. It was a grievous wrench to Benedict to tear himself away from all the ties of home; it was hard to refuse her request. In all his childish joys and sorrows he had turned for sympathy to that true and understanding heart, and she had never failed him.

So, in the darkness of the night, or in the hush of early morning, the two went forth together—Benedict the youth and the faithful woman who had nursed him in his childhood, and whose only plea was that she might serve him until death. Thus did Benedict refuse what the world could give him, lest in accepting he might lose his soul.

It was towards the Simbruini Mountains that he set his face, remembering, perhaps, the mountain peaks of his childhood's home in Umbria, and how they spoke to him of God. Along the Via Nomentana, hallowed by the footsteps of countless martyrs, passed the two wayfarers; past the church of St. Agnes, built by Constantine in the fourth century; to where the willow-fringed River Anio flows under the bridge over which Nero rode, when fleeing to his shameful death.

Having reached a place called Enfide, about two miles from Subiaco, they accepted the hospitality offered them by some kind Christians, who invited them to rest awhile before going further. Cyrilla, eager to prepare some refreshment for her companion, borrowed from the good neighbours the implements she needed, amongst them an earthenware sieve. Great was her distress when she found that the borrowed vessel, placed perilously near the edge of the table, had fallen and was broken in two. Her tears and lamentations touched the heart of Benedict, who, taking the broken pieces in his hands, knelt down and began to pray. His prayer ended, he found that the sieve was whole and entire, with no sign of the breakage, whereupon with comforting words he restored it to his nurse. Cyrilla made no secret of the marvel, and the people of the place, rejoicing that God had sent a Saint to dwell among them, came in crowds to visit him.

But it was not for this that Benedict had left his home. He had torn himself, as he thought, from the world and all that it could offer him; but love had followed him, and honour was laying snares for his feet. A long and weary fight lay before him if he was to conquer his own spirit, and it was a battle that must be waged alone, in solitude and silence. The grain of wheat must fall into the earth and die before it could bring forth the harvest that was to stay the world's hunger. For the souls of men, whether they know it or not, are always hungry for God, and the husks of the swine are but a sorry nourishment. Turning his back, therefore, on Cyrilla and the simple folk who were already prepared to venerate him as a Saint, Benedict set out alone for the desert. The first stage of the combat was at an end.

# CHAPTER 3

# BENEDICT IN THE DESERT

Crossing the little ridge of hills which lies between Enfide and the rocky gorge of the Anio, Benedict came to the spot where, more than four hundred years before, the Emperor Nero had dammed the swift waters of the river to form an artificial lake in the grounds of the stately villa which he had built for himself in that wild and beautiful valley. The villa had long since fallen into ruins; but the place, lonely and deserted now save for a few peasants and hermits who made their home amongst the rocks, was still known by the name that the wicked Emperor had given it— Sublaqueum, or "below the lake."

Now it happened that a certain monk named Romanus had chosen this quiet spot for meditation. Seeing a young man whose dress and appearance showed him to be of noble birth, and supposing that he had lost his way amongst the mountains, he courteously enquired of him whither he was bound. Benedict, looking into the friendly face of the questioner, whose grave eyes were bent on him with such a kindly sympathy, answered simply that he did not know. God had called him to a life of prayer and solitude, and he was seeking a place where he could fulfil his vocation.

Romanus was a holy man and well versed in the things of God. Entering into conversation with the young stranger, he soon learnt from him the story of his hasty flight from Rome, and the circumstances which had led up to it—a story which convinced him that he had to do with a chosen soul, for whom God had a secret mission. Acceding to the prayers of Benedict that he would give him the monastic habit, and show him some lonely place where he might live a hermit's life, Romanus clad him in the rough tunic of a monk, and led him to a hollow cave in the rocks, the existence of which was known to himself alone. So difficult indeed was it of access that the most enthusiastic explorer might have been discouraged in his search. From beneath it could only be approached by a laborious scramble over rocks and brushwood, while its roof was formed by a high and almost perpendicular rock. It was a depressing and lonely dwelling-place for so young an anchorite, shut in as it was on every side by the frowning mountains, in a silence broken only by the murmur of the river flowing in its rocky gorge beneath; but Benedict had found what he wanted, and was content.

The monastery where Romanus lived was several miles away; but the holy monk was mindful of the soul which God had, in a certain measure, confided to his care. Having promised that he would keep Benedict's secret, he could only visit him at dusk, when none could see where he went, and the daily portion of bread that he brought him was the half of his own repast. From the top of the precipice he would let it down in a basket, to which was attached a little bell, whose cheery tinkle called Benedict from his prayers to his only meal. "But the Evil One," says St. Gregory the Great, "envying the charity of one brother and the refreshment of the other, threw a stone one day and broke the bell," and henceforth, though Romanus continued to minister to the wants of his young friend, the voice of the little messenger was silent.

So the time flowed on; but Benedict had lost sight of days and hours, of times and seasons. Lost in the contemplation of God, he was learning many things that are taught in that divine school of prayer alone, a knowledge that was to fit him for the work for which God had set him apart.

It was Holy Week; and about three years had passed since his meeting with Romanus, when the visits of the latter suddenly ceased. He may have been ill; or obliged to go on a journey, and, being bound by his promise of secrecy, was unable to provide for Benedict during his absence. However that may be, we can be sure that he prayed that God would take care of his young charge; and we know that his prayer was answered. Moreover, the time had come when the ministry of Benedict was to begin, and God had His own ways of bringing this about:

There lived some miles from Subiaco a good priest who had a tiny parish in the neighbourhood. He was too poor to keep a servant, and on the evening of Holy Saturday had set to work to prepare himself a dinner that should be worthy of the Easter festival. That night Our Lord appeared to him in a vision. "while you have been preparing good things for your own dinner to-morrow," He said, "a servant of Mine is dying of hunger in a cave at Subiaco."

The priest arose at dawn, and, as soon as the Easter Mass was ended, set off towards the mountains, carrying with him the provisions he had prepared. Over the rocks and through the brushwood he scrambled, weary and breathless, searching for the holy man. At last, God guiding his footsteps, he reached the mouth of the cave, and greeting Benedict with joy and gladness, told him how God had revealed to him the place of his retreat.

After they had prayed and talked for some time together, the priest invited his companion to share with him the food that he had brought. "It is Easter Day," he said, "when it is fitting that men should feast." "Easter Day indeed," replied Benedict with sweet courtesy, "since I have merited to look upon your face." Thus did he practise what became afterwards a rule of his Order to greet all strangers as if they were Christ Himself. But the priest explained to him that it was in verity the Feast of the Resurrection, and on that account it was not becoming to fast. "It is for that reason," he added, "that God Himself has sent me to share with thee these His gifts."

Then the two men, having blessed the repast, partook of it together, discoursing the while of spiritual things, until it was time for the good priest to return to his flock. On his homeward way he mused on all that he had seen and heard; on the strange life of Benedict, his wonderful holiness, and the marvellous manner in which he himself had been led to seek him. It is probable that he spoke of these things to the humble peasants to whom he ministered, for shortly afterwards a little band of shepherds found their way to the cave. Seeing Benedict clothed in skins, and kneeling motionless in prayer, they took him for some wild beast of the forest, and at first did not dare to approach. But the sound of their footsteps disturbed the Saint, who turned towards them such a heavenly face that they stood as if spellbound, gazing at him with the greatest veneration. Such, indeed, was the charm of that beauty of holiness, that some of these rough and brutal men from that very moment changed their way of life. The words which Benedict addressed to them, simple teaching suited to their simple minds, were as sweet as his face, so that it is not surprising that people began to flock to the cave from all the country round, thinking it a privilege to be allowed to bring the necessaries of earthly life to him from whom they had received the message of the life that is eternal.

But the Evil One was watching jealously God's preparation of the Saint for his great mission, and made a desperate attempt to mar the work. He conjured up before Benedict's eyes the image of a beautiful young girl whom he had known in Rome, and who had perhaps been destined by his parents for his future bride. With the lovely vision came the thought of the life of ease and pleasure that he might be living, the joys of that world that he had abandoned, the weary hardships of the life which he had chosen. So strong was the temptation that he had almost yielded almost left the solitude of Subiaco and set his face towards the life and love that awaited him in Rome, when, throwing himself into a thicket of thorns and briers, he cured by the wounds of the body the wounds of the soul, and the temptation departed for ever.

The fame of the young Saint had spread meantime throughout the whole valley, and a community of monks who had a convent at Varia, now Vicovaro, twenty miles from Subiaco, and who had lately lost their Abbot, went in a body to ask Benedict to rule over them. The Saint had perhaps heard that their mode of life was no credit to their profession, or perhaps, with the strange intuition which was characteristic of him in later life, he was able to read their hearts. "Your ways and mine will never agree," he answered, refusing their request. But the monks would not accept his refusal; they desired reform, they said; and Benedict reluctantly, and hoping perhaps to lead them to better things, yielded at last to their persuasions. What he had undertaken to do he did conscientiously, insisting that they should obey their Rule and observe religious discipline; but this was not to their taste, and their desire for reform soon died out in angry murmuring, while each blamed the other for having conceived the mad idea of making such a man their Abbot. The very holiness of Benedict, a daily reproach to their own lives, served only to embitter their hatred, and their discontent at last reached its climax in a plot to poison the man whom they had induced, against his will, to put himself at their head.

This wicked plan, however, was doomed to failure. When the poisoned cup was presented to Benedict in the refectory, he blessed it with the sign of the Cross, whereupon it fell asunder in the hands of the bearer and the wine was spilt upon the ground. Realizing the meaning of the miracle, and reading their guilt in the pale and terrified faces of the monks, Benedict addressed them with his usual quiet calm.

"May God forgive you, my brethren," he said; "why have you plotted this wicked thing against me? Did I not say to you that your ways and mine would never agree? Seek now for another Abbot after your own heart, for you can keep me here no longer." With these words he went out from amongst them, and returned to his beloved solitude.

Monasticism in the West was a force which had not yet been organized, although more than one hundred years had passed since St. Athanasius came to Rome all on fire with the fervour of the holy lives of the monks of the East. His life of St. Anthony, the Father of Eastern monasticism, had been translated into Latin, and many had hastened to embrace the religious life on the lines of the Eastern observance. But the climate of Italy was very different from that of Northern Africa; the Rule of St. Pachomius and St. Anthony was hardly practicable in a colder country; relaxation had crept in and the standard had been lowered, for there was no fixed rule binding on all. Monks could go from one convent to another when they chose—a source of much disorder while the fervour of each house depended almost entirely on its Abbot. The monastic system in the west was waiting for the man who could adapt it to the needs of a colder climate, and, by giving it a special and definite form, make of it an instrument for the civilization of the nations, and that man was Benedict of Nursia.

# CHAPTER 4
# MAURUS AND PLACID

I t was not to the old hermit life at Subiaco that St. Benedict had returned, his fame had spread too far abroad for that. There were other monks in the valley besides those of Varia, men of a different stamp, seeking God in the simplicity of their hearts, but living under no particular rule, and with no definite aim in their religious life. For such men as these, when they came to put themselves under his guidance, Benedict had no refusal. There were others, too, rough barbarians and simple dwellers in the valley, who, desiring to give themselves to God, were seeking for one to lead them in His ways.

All these, like fatherless children, came thronging to Benedict, and thus was formed the nucleus of the Order that was to regenerate the world.

House after house was built, as the need arose for further accommodation, until there were twelve small monasteries under the Saint's direction. At the head of each of them was a Prior or Abbot of his own choosing, who could have recourse to him in every difficulty. Benedict himself lived at the

monastery of St. Clement's with a few chosen
monks who were to be the living embodiment of
his ideals, and to whose spiritual formation he devoted himself unceasingly. Over this large family he
ruled well and wisely, a living example to his
monks of what their lives should be, and gaining
the experience of men and matters that was to find
expression later in the Rule of his Order.

So did the wilderness begin to blossom as the
rose, and, as the fame of the monks of Subiaco
began to spread abroad, men came from all parts of
Italy to see the man who had done such wonders.
The memory of the boy of noble name and nature
who had fled from Rome to dedicate himself to God
in the desert had not died out in the old capital, and
many Romans went to Subiaco to see Benedict and
ask his advice. Among them came a nobleman
named Tertullus, who held the dignity of patrician,
and belonged probably to the same family as the
Saint. He was married to a good and fervent Christian like himself, and had four children whom he
brought up in the love of God and charity to the
poor. Arriving at Subiaco, clad in the magnificent
robes of his office, his first action was to kneel
down humbly at Benedict's feet, earnestly begging
him to ask God to pardon him his sins. A warm
friendship soon sprang up between these kindred
souls, and before Tertullus left Subiaco he had obtained a promise from Benedict to accept and bring
up in the ways of God his eldest son Placid, then
seven years old.

Another young disciple was also offered to the
Saint by Equitius, a Roman senator, in the person of
his son Maurus, a youth of riper years, remarkable
already for his wisdom and purity of heart, and des-

tined to be Benedict's greatest helper in the work
which lay before him. To him Benedict revealed his
hopes and his ideals the foundation of an Order
which was to adapt monasticism to the Western
world, and to bring the barbarian nations within
the fold of the Church.

The first thing that he taught to this dearest of
his sons was the value of prayer, and the efforts of
the Evil One to hinder it. To this end he took him
one day to one of the monasteries, where lived a
monk who was in the habit of leaving the chapel
during the time set apart for prayer, to wander
about the house and occupy himself with other
matters. His Superior had complained of this to the
Saint, who rebuked the man severely. For a short
time things went better; but ere long Benedict
heard that the culprit had fallen back again into his
old ways. "We will look into this," he said, and,
taking Maurus with him, went to the monastery,
where they knelt together in the chapel.

The brethren were assembled at prayer, and it
was not long before the Saint beheld a mysterious
black figure pulling at the monk's habit, who, in the
end, succeeded in dragging him out of the oratory.

"Do you see who leads him?" asked Benedict of
Maurus and of the Abbot, who was beside him.

"No," they answered.

"Pray then," said the Saint, "that your eyes may
be opened, and pray earnestly." Two days later
Maurus, kneeling in the same place in prayer, saw
in his turn the vision vouchsafed him at Benedict's
petition, that he might learn how hateful to the Evil
One is the regular monastic prayer, and how strong
are his temptations against it. "Take this rod and
strike the monk," said Benedict, giving Maurus his

staff, and at the first touch of it the enemy departed.

Nor was the little Placid without a like training; he, too, was to learn in a miraculous manner the power of prayer.

Three of St. Benedict's twelve monasteries were built on the rocky mountain side, and the monks had to fetch their water from the lake in the valley. Their lives were spent in climbing up and down the rocks. They complained one day to Benedict, that the work was beyond their strength. "Build us monasteries further down, O Father," they begged; but Benedict, while comforting them with the gentle sympathy that made him so beloved, returned no answer.

That night, when all were sleeping, he arose, roused the little Placid, and, taking him by the hand, led him to the crest of the rock on which the monasteries were built. "Let us pray," he said, and they knelt together.

The stars shone down on the wild mountain summit; the silence of the blue Italian night enfolded them the man kneeling motionless and rapt in prayer, and the little child, with angelic face turned heavenwards, nestling at his side. At last the Saint arose, and laying three stones one upon the other, took his small disciple by the hand and returned to the monastery.

The next day the monks complained again.

"Go to the top of the mountain," replied Benedict, "and in the place where you shall find three stones laid together, pierce the rock. Cannot God Almighty by His power give you water from the top of the mountain and relieve you of your weary toil?" No sooner had the rock been pierced than an abundant stream of water gushed out, sufficient for all the needs of the brethren.

Not only those of noble birth but men of all conditions were, as we have seen, received in the monasteries of Subiaco. When the barbarians, those terrible conquerors of his country, rough, poor, and ignorant, came to St. Benedict, they were welcomed as warmly as the wealthy and refined. Thus it happened that a poor Goth, coming one day and begging to be clothed in the habit of a monk, was received with joy by the Saint, who, giving him an axe, set him to clear away the thorns and briers from a piece of land beside the lake.

The muscular Goth put his heart into the work, and hacked away with such goodwill that the head of the axe flew off and was lost in the water.

Horrified at what he had done, the poor barbarian ran up to the monastery, and falling at the feet of the first person he met, who happened to be Maurus, confessed his fault with many tears. His distress was reported to Benedict, who spoke to him kindly and went with him down to the lake. Taking the handle of the axe from the poor novice, he held it out over the water; when, to the awe and astonishment of the Goth, the head rose from the bottom of the lake and fastened itself in its place. "Go now, my son," said Benedict, "and work, and be sad no longer, for when monks work hard, tools are often spoilt or broken."

God had already begun to reveal to St. Benedict, as He was so often to do in later years, the danger that threatened those whom he loved. One day the little Placid, having gone down to the lake to draw water, over-balanced himself and fell in.

"Brother Maurus," cried Benedict, "run quickly

to the lake and help the child, who is in danger of being drowned."

Kneeling hastily for his Father's blessing, Maurus ran down the mountain side, to find that the current had carried Placid far out of his depth. Thinking only of obeying the command he had received, the young monk ran out and seized the child by the hair, not perceiving until they were both on dry land that he had been walking on the water.

Trembling he went to tell the Saint of the wonder.

"The miracle was wrought by your obedience," said Benedict.

"Nay, Father, but by your command and through your prayers," was the answer. But the little Placid, who was listening, decided the question. "when I was being carried away," he said, I saw the cowl of my Father the Abbot over my head, and this it was that drew me out of the water."

Amongst the monks of Subiaco there was holiness and peace; but God has decreed that His followers must suffer persecution. Near to the monastery of St. Clement there lived a priest called Florentius, who was devoured with bitterness and jealousy at the sight of its prosperity. He was a bad man, and covetous of the presents which were offered to Benedict, as well as of his reputation for holiness. Florentius himself had tried to pose as a Saint, hoping for the same results, but nothing had come of it; his worldly and self-indulgent life was known to all, and the pretence was seen through at once. If the real Saint could be got rid of, he thought to himself, he might have a better chance; so, poisoning a small loaf, he sent it to Benedict as a friendly token of peace and charity.

The Abbot received the present courteously, but, as had happened once before, he was made aware of the danger. Calling a crow who came to feed every day from his hand

for all the wild creatures of the forest were his friends he bade it take the loaf in its beak and hide it where no one could find it. A few hours later, the bird, having executed his command, came back to receive its share of Benedict's frugal meal; but the Saint was sad at heart, thinking of Florentius's sin.

Disappointed in his attempt on Benedict's life, the unworthy priest conceived an infamous plan against the souls of the young monks under his care, sending women of evil life into the monastery garden to entice them from their work and prayers.

That his beloved sons should suffer danger on his account was more than Benedict could bear. Realizing that he and he alone was the cause of this bitter persecution, he determined to leave Subiaco and seek a dwelling-place elsewhere. The hatred of Florentius, although it probably hastened his departure, was not his only motive. Assembling the brethren together, he made known to them that Christ had commanded him to go to' Monte Cassino, to destroy there the worship of idols.

"Since this is so," continued the Saint, "I must obey and depart. You then remain here and stand firm in the grace and the holy life of religion, knowing that as you remain steadfast in this world, so shall it be with you in the world to come." Then, having set all things in order, and taking with him a few monks, among whom were his dear disciples Maurus and Placid, he set out for Monte Cassino.

Now the news that he had succeeded at last in driving out the Saint reached the ears of Florentius, who, exulting greatly, climbed to the balcony of his house to watch the little procession departing. But his triumph was short-lived, for, even as he stood there rejoicing, the balcony gave way, and the wicked priest was buried in its ruins.

It was not long before the monks of St. Clement's heard what had happened, and one of them, running with all haste after their departing Abbot, succeeded in overtaking the little company, ten miles away from Subiaco.

"Come back, O Father," he cried joyfully, "for the priest thine enemy is dead!"

But Benedict, severely rebuking him for his joy, continued on his way, lamenting bitterly the evil death of Florentius.

# CHAPTER 5

# MONTE CASSINO

Although Florentius was dead, for Benedict there was no turning back towards St. Clement's; the will of God was calling him elsewhere. But in the monasteries of Subiaco there was mourning and lamentation for the Father who would return no more to his sons. "The mountain grew pale with its own white mist; the caverns wept with grief; the wind wailed through the trees of the forest; the very waters of the lake moaned with anguish; even the wild beasts grieved for the loss of the man who was the friend of all the creatures of God, "wrote Mark the poet-monk. But the crows, who had been wont to share the frugal meals of the Saint and to feed from his hand, refused to be abandoned and went with him on his journey, flying before the little party as Heaven sent guides to show them the way to their destination.

At the monastery of St. Sebastian, near Alatri, the pilgrims stopped to rest, Servandus the Abbot, who had heard much of St. Benedict, receiving them with the greatest joy and hospitality. From thence along the valley of the Liris, they came to the province of Campania, celebrated in earlier times as one of the most fertile and flourishing regions of the Roman Empire. But the days of its prosperity had long since passed away. Devastated by incursion after incursion of barbarian armies, there was little to be seen, when Benedict and his monks first set foot in the country, but desolation and decay. Through the midst of it led the great Latin way, over which had streamed the Gothic hosts of Alaric, Odoacer, and Theodoric, and the Vandal hordes of Gaiseric. The inhabitants, flying in terror before the savage invaders, had taken refuge in the mountains, leaving the cultivated country to revert to marshland and wilderness.

The Roman town of Cassinum or Cassino, which had been celebrated for its fine buildings, its many inhabitants, and its noble families, lay on the mountain side near the Latin way, looking down on the smiling valley of the Liris. At the coming of St. Benedict in A.D. 529 it was deserted and partly in ruins, while there remained of its many inhabitants only a rustic population, living in the mountain fastnesses under continual terror of fresh invasion. The city had been Christian since Apostolic times, St. Peter, according to tradition, having sent it its first Bishop; but during the terrible years of the barbarian conquests it had fallen back into paganism.

The mission of St. Benedict was to bring these strayed sheep back into the fold of Christ; it was as the messenger of the Gospel that he came amongst a people stunned and terrified by misfortune. For the pagan Monte Cassino was destined to be the cradle of a Christian civilization that was to, spread through all the countries of Europe an ideal that was to last even to the present day.

St. Benedict seems to have been well received

by the Cassinese, pagans though they were. This, however, may have been partly owing to the fact that he came amongst them as owner of the land on which their city stood. It had been given to him by the patrician Tertullus, to whom it originally belonged, and who probably hoped by this dona-tion to redeem it from idolatry. It was in the spirit of apostles that the little band of monks set about their work, striving to draw men to Christ both by word and by example.

The mountain heights, which rose above the city, were clothed with magnificent forests, sacred to the worship of the heathen gods, to whom the people still offered sacrifice. On the highest crest, surrounded with walls and towers part of the an-cient defences of the city stood a temple dedicated to Apollo. From thence a sacred grove led to an altar where sacrifices were offered to the same deity. Further down the mountain side was a still older wall, dating from prehistoric times, and consisting of enormous blocks of stone flanked by a rudely constructed tower.

At the first sight of this stronghold of idolatry Benedict knelt on the rocks and prayed, foreseeing that the task which lay before him would be no easy one. Yet the teachings of Christianity were not quite extinct in the hearts of the people of Cassinum; and there were a good many amongst them who re-ceived the Saint as a father, following him wherever he went, lest they should lose a word of his teach-ing. These were the first-fruits of his prayers; but there still remained the greater number of the peo-ple, sunk in idolatry and paganism. To the eyes of Benedict, enlightened by long years of communing with God, many things were clear that were hidden from the sight of his disciples. He knew that the work which lay before him was destined to be the seed of a great enterprise and was not to be lightly undertaken.

It was the beginning of the holy season of Lent, a fit time for prayer and penance. Shutting himself up in the rude tower which gave entrance to the lower and older wall of the city, Benedict prepared himself, after his Master's example, for the ministry which lay before him. The first converts of the Saint, whose hearts he had already won, were greatly distressed at this sudden withdrawal. They besieged the tower, says the old chronicle, earnestly beseeching their newly-found teacher to show himself once more amongst them.

Their lamentations were in vain. It was not until the sacred Easter day had dawned that Benedict at last came forth from his retreat, chanting the Alleluia of the Paschal feast. The joyful cry was taken up by the monks and re-echoed by the faithful who stood without the tower. Then, with the Cross held on high before them, Benedict and his little band of disciples, followed by those of the townspeople who had been won to Christ by his preaching, ascended the mountain side to where, within the walls of the citadel, stood the ancient temple of Apollo. Entering the sacred grove where the pagans were wont to offer their sacrifices, the monks set to work to cut down the trees, which were to serve later for the building of the monastery.

This done, they proceeded to the crest of the mountain, where stood a great statue of the god on a column of Parian marble. Casting it down from its pedestal, the Saint planted the Cross they were carrying in its place; and on the site of the altar of sacrifice, which they also overthrew, they set to work to build an oratory which was to be dedicated to St. John the Baptist. The temple itself, having been purified and blessed by Benedict, became a Christian church under the protection of St. Martin of Tours. The mountain thus cleansed of its pagan associations, Benedict set to work to preach Christianity in the surrounding country.

But in this devastated spot, where terror of the barbarian went hand in hand with pagan superstition, there was one soul who had remained faithful to his God. This was a holy hermit called Martin, who dwelt in a cave on the mountain which was given over to the worship of Apollo. Day and night his prayers had interceded for a backsliding people until, Benedict having come to Cassino, he felt that his mission was fulfilled.

It has been said that that arrival of the Saint and the work that he was to accomplish had been made known to the anchorite by revelation. Whether this was so or not, after having visited the man of God and asked his counsel, the hermit left his cave at Monte Cassino and retired to another at some distance from the city. There, wishing to increase his penance, he bound himself by an iron chain to the rock, so that he could not stir from the place where he had made his abode. This was an austerity of which St. Benedict did not approve; he therefore sent a message to the hermit by one of his disciples. "If thou art a servant of God," it ran, "let not a chain of iron hold thee, but the chain of the love of Christ."

The hermit at once unfastened his chain, although he lived and died without setting foot outside his cave. Some disciples who had gathered round him in his solitude he sent to Benedict, bidding them take him as their spiritual guide; they were the first vocations of Monte Cassino. For, as the poet-monk Mark says, "The temples of the living God were to be established where the idols had been overthrown, and Benedict was to make fruitful the sterile works of men by watering their arid hearts with the dew of salvation." "It is always through hard labour," he says, "that we aspire to perfect things, and the path is always narrow that leads to the happy life."

It was indeed a life of hard labour and of great privation that was led by the monks in those early days at Monte Cassino, while the monastery was building. No workmen were employed, for the monks wrought themselves in the intervals of preaching to the people. A few came from Subiaco to help in the great work that was to do so much for the salvation of souls; but Benedict alone was the architect and his disciples the builders. In the meantime they lived where the pagan priests of Apollo had dwelt, near the tower in the citadel which Benedict had made his home, going forth from time to time into the surrounding country to preach the faith.

The barren fields, too, had need of cultivation; the terrified country people had to be encouraged to repair the ravages wrought by the barbarians. With faith in Christ came confidence for the future. The fields became fertile once more under the busy hands that found something everywhere to be done for God; houses were rebuilt, some semblance of peace and prosperity began to appear in that desolate region. It was a faint foreshadowing of what the Order was to do for the world in the days to come.

# CHAPTER 6

# BUILDING THE ABBEY

The Abbey of Monte Cassino rose rapidly under the busy hands of the monks, but it was not likely that the enemy of all good would easily allow himself to be driven out of a district where he had obtained such power. Strange portents hindered the brethren in their work; the stones that they were trying to lift would suddenly become immovable, and remained so until Benedict blessed them with the sign of the Cross. A vision of flames burst out suddenly in the half-completed building and terrified the monks, who ran hither and thither seeking for water; but Benedict bade them sign their eyes with the holy sign, and there was no fire to be seen.

To the Saint himself the Evil One appeared in a terrible form, threatening and reviling him. "Not Benedict not blessed, but ac cursed art thou!" he cried; "why hast thou come to torment me?" A wall which the brethren were building fell suddenly, without apparent cause, burying in its ruins a young monk named Severus. This time it would have seemed that the spirit of evil had triumphed; and the builders, lifting the shattered and lifeless body of their companion in their arms, carried it to Benedict and laid it at his feet with no other comment than their tears. But the Saint, who was praying, redoubled his prayers; and presently the young workman went forth again to his labour as if nothing had befallen him.

The walls of the old citadel were used to form part of the monastery, and of the tower that flanked them St. Benedict made his own abode. It was divided into two stories: in the lower room he read, wrote, and received the many visitors who thronged to see him; while the upper one served him as oratory. The church of the monastery was the old temple of Apollo, which had been purified and dedicated to St. Martin of Tours. Within the enclosure there were dormitories for the monks, for the boys who were under their charge, and for the novices; cells for guests and for the poor; refectory, kitchen, workshops for different trades, and a library where the monks could read and study.

The newly-founded monastery was quickly filled; every day brought new disciples, who, rich or poor, gentle or simple, learned or ignorant, received the same welcome. All that St. Benedict asked was a humble and docile spirit, willingness to work, an earnest desire to love and serve God.

Associated with the Saint in the government of the house were his two dear disciples, Maurus and Placid, fit sons of such a Father, and beloved by all for their wisdom and holiness. Of Constantine, who lived long with St. Benedict and succeeded him as Abbot, we know nothing save that he was revered in the Order as a Saint, as were also Paulinus and Augustine, his companions. Among those who formed that first community at Monte Cassino were Simplicius and Faustus, who in after years went with St. Maurus into France; Mark the poet, who had followed his master from Subiaco; the brave little group who were later to set out with Placid into Sicily, there to meet the martyr's death; and Severus, the boy-monk who had been raised to life by the prayers of Benedict, and was henceforward loved by him with an especial tenderness.

The news of the transformation that had been brought about at Monte Cassino came in due time to the ears of Tertullus in Rome, who at once set out to visit the monastery. With him went Aequitius, the father of Maurus, and we can imagine with what joy they were welcomed by Benedict and his young disciples. Great was the consolation of Tertullus at the good work accomplished; he confirmed his gift of the land by charter, asking only that when his time came to die, he might be buried in the monastery. He made over also to the man of God a property which he possessed in Sicily, in the hope that a Benedictine monastery might be founded there.

It was well for the people of Campania that they had found a father in the Saint, and that Monte Cassino was a refuge for all who were in sorrow or distress, for the troubles of the country were by no means at an end. The Emperor Justinian had succeeded his uncle on the throne of the Eastern Empire, and the dream of his heart was to reconquer the Empire of the West. A brilliant young officer called Belisarius was winning renown at the head of his army, and Sicily had already fallen to his sword. The glorious Theodoric was dead; his successor was but a child. The moment seemed ripe to sweep the Goths beyond the barriers of the Empire,

and to unite it under one Caesar as of old. The conquering legions of Belisarius penetrated into Italy;
the Goths made a desperate resistance; plague and
famine followed in the footsteps of war. The
country people, reduced to the last extremity, died
by hundreds. Grass and acorns were eaten as food,
and ghastly tales were told of famished creatures
who fed on human flesh, and mothers who put
their own children to death rather than witness
their sufferings.

The poorer inhabitants of Campania besieged
the monastery begging for bread; nor did they beg
in vain. "Give, for the love of God," said Benedict,
"while there is anything left to give "; until there
came a day when there was nothing for the monks'
frugal meal. This, thought some of the brethren,
was carrying charity a little too far, and they gave
way to despondency, not fancying the prospect of
death by starvation. Benedict reproached them
gently for their want of confidence. "Are you trou-
bled at the lack of bread?" he asked; "true, there is
not much to-day, but there will be more to-
morrow."

The next day two hundred bushels of flour were
found at the monastery gate, the gift of an un-
known benefactor; and the monks who had complained gave thanks to God, resolving to put their
trust in His Providence for the future. It was not
only flour that was wanting, but everything else.
There came one day to the monastery a certain
deacon called Agapitus, who asked the monks if, for
the love of God, they could not give him a little oil.
Now there was no oil left in the cellar but a little
drop at the bottom of a small vessel, and the cellarer, being bidden to give that little store to Agapi-

tus, thought proper to pretend to be a little hard of hearing. On being asked shortly afterwards if he had obeyed Benedict's command, he excused himself by saying that he felt sure that there had been some mistake, since if he had given the oil there would not have remained a drop in the house.

"Bring the jar of oil here," said Benedict, "and throw it out of that window, lest what has been preserved through disobedience should bring a curse upon the house."

The crestfallen cellarer obeyed the Abbot's orders, and the jar fell upon the rocks beneath. "Go now," said the Saint, "turning to another monk, "and fetch the oil, and give it to Agapitus." The astonishment of the messenger was great when he found the vessel whole and the oil unspilt. Marvelling greatly, he climbed up the rock, and having given it to the subdeacon, returned to the Abbot's cell. Placing an empty jar in the middle of the floor, the Saint then bade the brethren kneel and pray fervently. As they did so, the oil rose to the lip of the vessel and flowed over on the ground; whereupon Benedict, having reproved the cellarer before them all for his disobedience and want of faith, exhorted him to show himself more trustful for the future.

It was not only food for the body but comfort for their sorrowing hearts that the people came to seek at Monte Cassino. A poor man who had lost his only son brought the little body in his arms to Benedict, asking that if it were the will of God he would restore the child to life by his prayers. The poor countryman was so breathless with weeping and his hurried climb up the mountain side, that he could only hold out his pitiful little burden and gasp the Saint's name. But a brother who met him understood well enough what he wanted. "He is working in the fields with the monks," he told him; and the man laying his child's body tenderly upon the ground at the monastery door, went to seek the Abbot. He had not gone far when he met the Saint returning with his monks to the house.

"Give me back my son, my little son," implored the poor father, falling at Benedict's feet; "he is dead, restore him to life." The man's despair touched the monks, who added their entreaties to his, but Benedict reproved them gravely. "Such deeds are for the holy Apostles," he answered, "and not for a man like me." But the child's father would take no denial. "I will not go away," he said, "till my son is restored to me; he is there at the gate of the monastery."

They went together to the spot, and Benedict, kneeling by the motionless little body, laid his hands upon it and raised his eyes to Heaven. "Regard not my sins, O Lord," he prayed, "but the faith of this man who implores Thee to give him back his child." Even as he spoke a tremor ran through the little body and the child breathed again. Raising him to his feet, Benedict gave him back to his father, and the two went down the mountain path hand in hand together.

Soon after the foundation of Monte Cassino, an assembly of holy women had gathered in the neighbourhood under the Rule and guidance of St. Benedict. Some of them lived in a monastery at Piumarola in the valley of the Liris, their Abbess being Scholastica, the beloved twin sister of St. Benedict, who, having dedicated herself from her earliest childhood to God, had come to Monte Cassino to live under her brother's direction. Others lived in twos or threes in their own houses, and having also consecrated themselves to the service of God, followed a definite rule.

Amongst these were two ladies of noble birth, who, though desirous of leading a holy life, had not quite succeeded in overcoming nature and the prejudices of the world. In order that they might be more free to follow their vocation, a certain good man, perhaps one of the monks of Monte Cassino, was deputed by St. Benedict to take them what they needed and to act in some sort as their servant. This individual, however, whether monk or layman, was of humble condition, and this the noble ladies could not forget. No longer able to bear their sharp words and contemptuous language, the poor victim at last complained to St. Benedict, who warned the two recluses that if they did not mend their ways and practise charity more perfectly, he would be obliged to ex-communicate them. Nature, however, prevailed over grace, and matters became worse instead of better. But the unfortunate man, who did his best to bear his troubles patiently, was destined to be soon delivered from his sharp-tongued persecutors. The two recluses died, and were buried in the precincts of the church.

Now it happened that their old nurse, who had lived with them, assisting at Mass and going up to the altar to offer the accustomed oblation for her two mistresses, saw a sight that filled her with fear. It was the moment when, before beginning the Canon of the Mass, the priest, turning to the congregation, ordered the catechumens and excommunicated persons to depart from the church. As the words left his lips, two shadowy figures arose from the newly made tomb, and stole silently out at the door. The same thing having occurred several times, the nurse in great distress went to Benedict and told him what she had seen. "Take this oblation," he said, "and offer it for them on my behalf." This was done; and the dead henceforward slept in peace.

# CHAPTER 7
# BENEDICT'S RULE

The great defect in the monastic life of the West before the time of St. Benedict was the want of unity. The Eastern Rule, not being adapted to the needs of a colder climate, was only partially kept, and each head of a religious house governed according to his own ideas. Some undertook too much, and, growing weary of a life of excessive austerity, cast away all restraint; whilst others allowed themselves so much liberty that they did small honour to their religious profession. Law and order in the monastic life were needed, and they were given to the world in the Rule of St. Benedict.

The Father of Western monasticism, as he has been called, had had a long experience of human nature; he knew its strength and its weakness, its aspirations, and its needs. He himself had practised great austerities in his cave at Subiaco, but he had realized that such a life was for the few rather than for the many. And the religious life, as he had dreamed of it, was to be for all, for every class of mind and for every degree of learning, for the educated and for the ignorant, for sinners and for

Saints. So with the wisdom that comes of experience and the understanding that comes of sympathy, he set to work to compile his Rule, the principles of which he had already put into practice in his government of the monasteries of Subiaco.

The monastery was to be, above all, a family; there was to be no distinction of rank or condition. No man of noble birth was to be preferred, on that account, before one who had been a slave; the sole distinction was to be personal merit. At the head of all, as father of the family, was the Abbot. To him all owed respect and obedience, an obedience that was to be prompt, cheerful, and unquestioning. He was to act as a true father, gentle with the weak, stern towards the rebellious, just towards all, ruling as the representative of Christ, rather by love than by fear. Chosen by the common consent of the monks, he was to be chaste, sober, and merciful. He was to act with prudence when correcting those beneath him, remembering that he, too, was human and subject to the frailties of human nature. He was to rule so that the strong might still have something to strive for, and the weak might have nothing to fear.

There were to be no excessive austerities; humility and obedience were to be the service of the Benedictine monk, and by the practice of these virtues he was to offer himself a living sacrifice to his God. The cloister was to be a school of useful workers, whose labours were sanctified by prayer; the bodies of the monks were to be kept healthy, that they might be more fit for both.

The long tunic and hood which formed the monastic dress were the ordinary working clothes of the people. Cleanliness was to be observed by all, and to be provided for by the authorities. The food, though simple, was to be sufficient to sustain the strength of men who were hard workers, for the life of the monks was one of labour, and they ate their bread literally in the sweat of their brow.

Idleness, as St. Benedict well knew, is the enemy of all good, and in the monastery there was work for all. Reading, study, manual labour, succeeded each other at regular intervals; the monks were in turn preachers, writers, historians, husbandmen, and workmen, as each had capacity. Even the infirm and the sick were to be encouraged to undertake some occupation adapted to their strength, that none, being idle, might fall an easy prey to temptation. Yet to the sick all tenderness was to be shown. "Let them be served in very deed as Christ Himself," says St. Benedict; and everything was to be done to make them contented and happy.

There was to be no "mine and thine" in the monastery, for everything was to be in common, and all that was necessary for the brethren was to come to them through the hands of the Abbot.

The great spiritual centre of monastic life was to be the public prayer in common, the recitation of the Divine Office, which was to be the fruitful source of strength, zeal, and inspiration. The day was so planned that work and prayer succeeded each other; but if the prayer was to be the "Work of God," the work was to be also a prayer.

No novice was received in the monastery until his virtue and perseverance had been put to the test. If, after having been two months in the house he was considered a suitable subject, the Rule was read to him. "Here is the law under which you desire to fight," they then said to him: "If you can keep it, remain; if not, you are free to depart."

It belonged to the Abbot to arrange that each one should have the work that was best suited to his abilities, and as everything used in the monastery was made by the monks, there was scope for every talent. Each department was under the care of a competent overseer who was responsible for everything that concerned it. That the monks were excellent workmen and husbandmen few people will dispute. They came to a bare and barren country and made it blossom like the rose. Mark the poet draws a picture of their work at Cassino in a poem, where he makes the mountain thank the Saint for all that he has done for it. "Thou changest the desert lands into smiling gardens, and coverest the barren mountain with fruitful shoots, and the rock marvels at the wheat crops and the fruits that are not its own, and the wood becomes green with waving apple-trees."

There are writers of the present day who are careful to point out to us how far from unworldly was the eagerness of the monks to select the most beautiful spots wherein to build their monasteries. The true state of things was very different. It was more often than not on the barest and most barren land that they settled, and in the sweat of their brow that they tilled the land and made it fruitful. In the days when slavery lay like a curse upon Europe and labour was considered a disgrace, Benedict the patrician, with Placid and Maurus and others of the noblest of the families of Rome, went forth to labour side by side with the son of the slave. "Let him that is the greatest among you be your servant," said their Master, and in the monastery that precept was obeyed.

But it is not only in the fertility of the land that the work of the monks has survived. By their patient labour in the scriptorium were preserved and handed down to future generations the treasures of classical literature and the only histories of the time that we possess. The Holy Scriptures, the works of the Fathers of the Church and many others, would have been lost to the world had it not been for their diligence; and it is from their chronicles chiefly that our knowledge of the Saints is drawn.

Many of the monks, by the Abbot's orders, devoted themselves to study, for among other things the monastery was a school. Boys and youths, as was the case with Maurus and Placid, were received into the house and educated, either for the religious life or for a worldly career. Teachers had to be provided for the young pupils, that they might learn to read and write, to interpret and to transcribe. Grammars and textbooks had to be compiled for their use, and multiplied by copying.

It was the custom in those days for parents to dedicate their children while still in early youth to the religious life. As the little Samuel was dedicated to the service of God by his pious mother, so did these good people bring their sons to the monastery. The little neophytes were offered before the altar; the sacred corporal was wrapped round their baby hands, and they became from henceforth one of the religious family. These infant novices brought an element of youthful gaiety into the monastery, they were brought up and instructed by the elder brethren, and they usually made good and fervent monks. They were the children of the house;

around it clustered all the sweetest memories of their early days; the Abbot was their father, the brethren their family.

St. Boniface, the Apostle of Germany, became a monk at five years old, our own St. Bede at seven. This was the age at which the little oblates began their education. Their first lesson book was the Psalter, which, as soon as they could read, they learnt by heart. Grammar followed, with the study of the Latin tongue and literature, not so difficult to them, since it was their native language. At fourteen those who were dedicated to the religious life began the studies necessary for a monk; while those who were destined for the world entered on their secular career. For the former, natural taste and capacity were taken into account. The higher education might consist of theology, medicine, mathematics, painting or music, sculpture or wood carving, while transcription was the most common study of all. Those of the monks who had no "book-learning" were trained in manual labour; but all lent a hand in the cultivation of the monastery lands.

The care of guests and pilgrims was entrusted to monks of tried virtue. They were to treat the guests who came to the monastery as if they were Christ Himself, remembering that He had said, "I was a stranger and ye took Me in." On their arrival their feet were washed by the Abbot, who took his meals with them and showed them every courtesy. The poor were to be treated with no less honour than the rich, since they were the especial representatives of Christ.

In the time of St. Benedict a continual stream of guests passed backwards and forwards from Monte

Cassino. Abbots of other religious houses came to seek his counsel; nobles and Bishops came to see the quiet, strong, peace-loving man who by his wisdom and keen power of sympathy had become the centre of the lives and interests of all around him. The poor and the destitute came to him for succour in their distress, the sinful and sorrowful for spiritual help. And all these, going their different ways in the world, spread abroad the fame of the holiness of the monks and the peace of the monastic life, which seemed to them like a foretaste of the peace of Paradise. And men who were weary of the world, with its sin, its turmoil and unrest, hearing of this oasis in the desert, came to offer themselves to Benedict as disciples, that they, too, might learn the way of peace. Even the barbarians, as we shall see later, felt themselves strangely attracted by they knew not what of unearthly magnetism, and in the presence of Benedict laid aside their savagery and became meek as little children. They were rough and unlearned, but their strong natures were capable of receiving the Christian faith. For "paganism, vanquished by the Cross, the subduer of the world, did not surrender itself to the discretion of a proud conqueror; it surrendered to Christ, who was meek and humble of heart."

# CHAPTER 8
## THE GIFT OF VISION

Of all the supernatural gifts which God has given to His Saints, perhaps that of being able to read the hearts of others is the most common. Though the understanding love and sympathy that comes from self-forgetfulness has no doubt its part in the matter, it cannot quite explain the mystery. St. Benedict, like most founders of a religious Order, possessed this gift in a remarkable degree, and many instances of its exercise are made known to us by his contemporaries.

One day when some of his monks had been obliged, as occasionally happened, to go out on business, they were not able to return until a later hour than usual. It was the rule that the brethren should take no meals outside the monastery; but on this occasion, feeling hungry, they had gone to the house of a Christian woman who was known to them and asked for refreshment. Delighted to be able to do the monks a service, the good housewife set before them the best that she had, and, after having appeased their hunger, they went their way homewards. On returning to the monastery they were met by the Saint, who asked them where they had refreshed themselves. Fearful of a reproof, they declared that they had taken nothing; whereupon Benedict quietly told them where they had been and what they had eaten. Falling at his feet, they asked his pardon, which was instantly granted. "But act uprightly in the future," he added, "for even when absent from you in the flesh I am present in the spirit."

A certain man who used to come every year to Monte Cassino to see his brother, who was a monk, had made the resolution never to break his fast on the journey. Being tempted one day, however, he gave way, to be gently reproached on his arrival by Benedict, who knew exactly what had passed. On another occasion one of the monks who was preaching to the nuns in a neighbouring convent, accepted at their request a present of handkerchiefs for his own use. As, however, the Rule forbade the acceptance of gifts, he hid them in the bosom of his tunic and presently forgot all about them. On his return to the monastery he was sent for by the Abbot, who asked him why he had been unfaithful to his Rule.

"Take out of your bosom and cast away from you," he said, "what has been the occasion of your fall."

One evening when Benedict was partaking of his frugal evening meal, there stood beside him, according to the custom of the house, a young monk whose duty it was to hold the lamp and to serve at table. Now it happened that this particular monk, who was of noble birth, began to rebel in his heart against the menial office he was performing. "Who is this man," he asked himself indignantly, "who sits and eats, while I, who should by rights be waited on by others, attend him like a slave?" In silence he fulfilled the duties of his office, a tempest of pride and anger in his heart; but his thoughts were as clear to Benedict as if they had been uttered aloud. "Sign thy heart with the Cross, my brother," he said in a voice of stern rebuke, "sign thy heart with the Cross; what is it that thou art saying? Sign thy heart with the Cross." Then bidding the young server give the lamp to one of his brethren, he sent him away for an hour of silent prayer, during which the novice fought with and overcame his temptation. On being asked by the others what had occasioned the unusually stern rebuke, the culprit told them the whole story. "There is no thought of our hearts that is hidden from the knowledge of our Father," he said, "they are all as spoken words to him."

The bravest warrior among the Goths at this time was the famous Totila, their King. A brilliant soldier and tactician, he was not without nobility of nature, although as an Arian he had persecuted many monks and priests of the Catholic Church. One of his followers, named Galla, was especially bitter against the Catholics, and had sworn to take the life of every monk he met. One day, when on a plundering expedition, he seized a poor peasant and ordered him to give up his possessions. The man, who was really penniless, maintained that he had nothing; but on being put to the torture, declared that he had given all he possessed into the keeping of Benedict, the Abbot of Monte Cassino. Binding him securely, the savage barbarian drove him before him to the monastery, that he might demand of the Saint the money that had been entrusted to his charge. Benedict, who was reading in the doorway of his cell, did not move at their approach.

"Get up," roared the Goth, "and give me this man's money." The Saint, then, lifting his eyes from his book, fixed them on the peasant, who stood trembling with fear at the thought of the punishment he deserved for his deception. At the glance of those steadfast eyes, the bonds which held him snapped as if they had been cut with a knife, and fell at his feet. It was now the turn of the Goth to tremble; but Benedict, without rising from his seat, called to his monks and bade them take the astonished Galla to the refectory that he might partake of refreshment and receive the blessing due to a guest. Nor was the blessing without its effect, for before he left the monastery the savage barbarian knelt at the feet of the Saint, and, having confessed his faults and listened humbly to his instructions, promised to amend his ways. The change in his behaviour did not escape the notice of his companions, and the whole story having been repeated to Totila, the King conceived a great desire to see the man who could work such wonders.

He had no intention, however, of taking the Saint's miraculous powers for granted. Having sent a messenger to Benedict to inform him that the Gothic King would shortly pay him a visit, Totila determined to test his reported insight by sending another in his place. Dressing up his sword-bearer Riggo in his royal armour and purple mantle, he bade him ride up to the monastery and announce himself as the King. In order that the deception might be complete, he bade three of his noblest courtiers who usually attended him wherever he went, to ride at the head of the guard of honour that was to act as escort.

Up the steep mountain road, with much tramping of horses and jingling of arms, rode the gay cavalcade, creating perhaps some little flutter of excitement in the silent monastery.

Benedict stood at the door of his cell, looking out with quiet eyes at the approaching company. No word did he speak until the mock king was ready to dismount, when he addressed him in stern accents. "Put off, my son," he said, "that which thou wearest, for it is not thine own." The unfortunate Riggo, terrified at the Saint's detection of the fraud, fell flat on his face before him, an example which the rest of the troop thought well to imitate. When they at length arose, it was not to come forward, but to gallop back with all possible speed to Totila with the news of the detection. The Gothic King, much impressed with their story, determined this time to go in person. Desiring to behave with the respect due to a Saint, he dismounted at a little distance from the monastery, and prostrated himself humbly before Benedict, who was again reading at the door of his cell. The Saint called out to him to rise; but, seeing he did not do so, went himself to meet him, raised him up, and led him to the monastery. Finding the King in such good dispositions, he began to reprove him gently for the evil he had done, and exhorted him to lead a better life in the future, while Totila, who seemed deeply moved and not a little frightened, listened humbly to what he had to say.

Then the Saint uttered the prophecy that—was to come so strangely true in every particular. "Thou shalt enter Rome," he said; "thou shalt cross the sea; nine years shalt thou reign, and in the tenth thou shalt die." At these words the barbarian King was more terrified than ever, and, having begged the prayers of Benedict, departed.

It was remarked of Totila that he was a changed man after the interview, and many beautiful tales are told of kindness shown to captives and mercy shown to enemies during the last ten years of his reign. Within the year, he defeated the forces of Justinian and became lord of Rome. In the tenth year after his interview with the Saint, he crossed to Sicily, and a few weeks later, in a battle with Narses, the general of the Emperor, lost both his life and his kingdom. It was the final defeat of the great Ostrogothic race, which as a nation disappears from history. Italy under Narses became an exarchate of the Empire of the East, and was governed by Byzantine law.

On several occasions St. Benedict foretold the things that were to happen after his death. He was talking one day with the Bishop of Canosa about the entrance of Totila into Rome. "The city will be so destroyed," lamented the Bishop," that it will be no more inhabitable." "Not so," answered the Saint; "it is not by the hand of the barbarians that Rome shall be ruined, but by tempests, lightnings, whirlwinds, and earthquakes," "which things," says St. Gregory the Great, writing some fifty years later, "we ourselves have seen."

On another occasion a monk of Monte Cassino called Theoprobus, chosen by the Saint on account of his holy life to be his familiar friend and confidant, entering the cell of the Abbot, found him weeping bitterly. Theoprobus having asked the cause of his tears, Benedict replied with many lamentations, "with care and labour have I built this monastery, and striven to make its inmates true servants of God, and now, behold God has made known to me that after my death it will fall into' the hands of the infidels; only by my prayers and supplications have I succeeded in obtaining that the lives of the brethren should be spared." St. Gregory again bears witness to the truth of the prophecy, for, during his lifetime, the monastery of Monte Cassino was destroyed by the Lombards, who entered it during the night while the monks were asleep. Yet, though they destroyed everything on which they could lay their hands, not one of the brethren perished. Protected by the prayers of the Saint, they fled from their mountain retreat and found shelter in the city of Rome. It was here that St. Gregory the Great learnt from the monks who had been the intimate companions of the Saint, the story of his life and miracles, and, reading his Rule, was so entranced by its wisdom that he himself embraced it.

CHAPTER 9
# SPREADING THE ORDER

The time had come when Maurus and Placid, the most beloved of St. Benedict's disciples, were to carry the Rule of their master into other countries. The first foundation was to be in Sicily, on the land which had been given to the Saint by the patrician Tertullus when he came to visit him at Monte Cassino. Was it for this reason that the son of Tertullus was chosen for the mission, or was it that Benedict, knowing the fruitfulness of a good work which is rooted in sacrifice, chose deliberately to separate himself from what was most dear to him on earth? We do not know. That Placid was pre-eminently fitted for the work was proved by the unanimous consent of the brethren when the Saint proposed him for the undertaking.

As the hour of parting drew near, Benedict comforted his sorrowing disciple with inspiring words, bidding him enter with a stout heart on the great mission which lay before him, and prophesying that he would win the martyr's crown. In the spring of the year 537 he set forth on his journey, accompanied by the little band of monks who were to

carry the traditions of their founder into Sicily.
Their first halt was at Capua, where Germanus the
Bishop, an intimate friend of St. Benedict's, received them with cordial hospitality. At Canosa
they were entertained by another warm admirer of
their holy Abbot; everywhere they went the sons of
such a Father were received with open arms.

No sooner had they arrived at Messina than
Placid set to work at the foundation of the new
monastery; but little is known of his apostolate in
the island. He was martyred, as St. Benedict had
foreseen, during an invasion of the barbarians.
With him perished two of his brothers and his
sister Flavia, who had come from Rome to pay him
a visit, together with the greater number of the
monks. When St. Benedict received the news of the
death of this first martyr of the Order, he burst out
into thanksgiving that it had been granted to his
beloved Placid to give his life for the Faith.

The mission of Maurus was to be yet further
afield. While Benedict was still a youth pursuing
his studies at his father's house in Rome, the pagan
King of the Franks, Chlodovech or Clovis, had married Clotilda, the niece of Gundobad, King of Burgundy. Clotilda's mother had been a fervent
Catholic, whose gentle influence on her Arian husband had induced him to allow her to bring up her
children in the Catholic faith.

Clovis was at this time engaged in fighting with
the powerful tribes of the Alemanni, and for some
time resisted the entreaties of his wife that he
would renounce paganism and embrace the
Catholic faith. But the day dawned when, facing a
powerful army of his foes, the Frankish King realized that on the battle that was about to be fought

rested his whole hope of sovereignty. Recalling to mind the earnest words of his wife, he uttered his first Christian prayer. "Oh, Jesus Christ," he cried, "whom Clotilda declares to be the Son of the living God, and who art said to give help to those who are in trouble if they trust in Thee, I humbly beseech Thy assistance. I have called on my gods and they are far from my help. If Thou wilt deliver me from mine enemies I will believe in Thee and be baptized in Thy Name." The result of the battle was a complete triumph for the King of the Franks, who, returning to his wife, received baptism in the Cathedral at Rheims on Christmas Day, 496, at the hands of the Archbishop, St. Remigius.

"Bow thy head," said the holy Archbishop to his royal convert as he stood before the font, "and burning what thou hast adored, adore what thou hast burned."

The consequences of his conversion were great. The sword of the most powerful ruler in Europe was henceforward to be drawn in defence of the true Faith, while the whole Frankish nation abjured paganism, and France became a Catholic country. It takes time, however, to win a barbarian people, but lately steeped in paganism, to Catholic faith and practice. It is not surprising, therefore, that some forty years later we find Innocent, Bishop of Mans, writing to Benedict to beg him to send some of the most experienced of his monks to found a monastery of his Rule in Gaul.

Although Maurus had been for long his right hand in the government of Monte Cassino, Benedict resolved once more to call down the grace of God on the enterprise by making the sacrifice of this beloved son. The hearts of the brethren were sore at the thought of losing one who was so much beloved by them all, but they could not but agree with their holy Abbot that the wisdom and holiness of Maurus pointed him out as the fittest among them for the work. Yet Maurus, who, after the example of his holy Father, generously accepted the sacrifice, could not altogether conceal his grief at the thought of the parting, a grief which was universally shared.

The tears and lamentations of the brethren touched the heart of the Abbot, who, forgetting his own sorrow at the sight of theirs, tried his best to comfort them. "Since charity is kind, most dearly beloved sons and brothers," he said, "we are bound by it to show kindness to all who are in need of it, and to desire the good of others rather than our own. I beg you, therefore, by the fatherly love I bear you, to restrain your tears and sadness. Let us beware lest that which to others is a cause of salvation, may become to some of us, through excess of grief, an occasion of loss. Know also, that we who are bound together by the holy bond of charity cannot be separated by distance, for in Christ we ever are, and ever shall be, one."

Then turning to the little band of monks who had been chosen to go to France with Maurus, "You, most dear brethren," he said, "who are going forth to work for God in a distant land, act manfully and be strengthened. The more you suffer for souls the greater will be your reward. And grieve not at the thought that my death must be close at hand, for when I shall have laid aside this mortal body I shall be nearer to you than ever, and more powerful by God's grace to help you."

Brave and hopeful words, but the heart of the

old man went out with a wistful tenderness after the travellers. Having led them as far as the monastery gate, he blessed them and bade them a last farewell, watching them through eyes that were dim with tears, as with heavy hearts they descended the mountain path.

Their first stopping place was Aquinum, where they were to spend the night at a house belonging to the monastery, and here they found another token of their Father's fostering care. Two monks had been sent on before-hand from Monte Cassino to prepare for their reception and to give them a hospitable welcome. Nor was this all. At daybreak next morning, as they were about to continue their journey, a little deputation consisting of two young monks, of whom one, Felicissimus, was the cousin of St. Maurus, came to wish them a last godspeed, bringing with them some small mementoes of Monte Cassino and a letter from St. Benedict.

"Accept, most beloved," the Saint had written, "this last gift of thy master, as a token of his enduring love of thee." Then, after having prophesied that Maurus would pass through many tribulations, during which he would be sustained by the goodness of God, he announced that he would enter into the joys of heaven after sixty years spent in the religious life: "Mayest thou be happy," he prayed, "in thy going forth, and still more happy in thy end."

Filled with joy and consolation at the thought that the heart and the prayers of the Saint were with them, the little party set out once more on their journey, Maurus having first taken his young cousin apart and exhorted him to be faithful to his vocation.

The first Benedictine monastery in Gaul was founded at Glanfeuil in Anjou. St. Maurus was its Abbot till the year 581, when he died in the odor of sanctity.

Several other foundations were made in Italy during the lifetime of St. Benedict. Besides the monasteries of Subiaco and Monte Cassino, he presided over that of Terracina, built on the property of a holy man who had begged the Saint to send some of his monks to found there a religious house. Others were built on the various properties given by Tertullus to the Saint. It was in a Benedictine monastery on the island of Ponza that Belisarius, at the command of the wicked Empress Theodora, imprisoned Pope St. Silverius, who was later to die the martyr's death. Another monastery, erected during the lifetime of Benedict at Novalesa in Piedmont, was ruined by the Lombards about the same time as that of Monte Cassino. In another, situated in Perugia, lived the monk St. Herculanus, who became Bishop of the city and was murdered by the Goths.

The destruction of the Abbey of Monte Cassino some forty years after St. Benedict's death, which might have destroyed as well the work of a lifetime, seemed, through the providence of God, rather to assist its development. The Abbot and those of the monks 99) ?> who had fled to Rome to seek the protection of Pope Pelagius II. took up their abode temporarily in the monastery of the Lateran, where they spread the traditions and the teaching of their Founder. It was here, as we have seen, that Gregory, the scion of a noble Roman family, and afterwards Pope St. Gregory the Great, took the Benedictine habit, and so became the first of the sons of St. Benedict to wear the Papal tiara.

A few monks, however, when the Abbey of Monte Cassino was sacked by the Lombards, concealed themselves among the mountains, to return, after the first force of the invasion had spent itself, to their ruined monastery, where they remained faithful guardians of the tomb of their holy Founder. A little more than a hundred years later Petronax, a certain pious citizen of Brescia, who had come to Rome to venerate the tombs of the Apostles, spoke to the Pope of his desire to help in the restoration of Monte Cassino. His suggestion having been received with enthusiasm, he set out at once for the ruined Abbey, where he found a few anchorites living in the greatest poverty. The work of restoration progressed satisfactorily, and in due time Petronax, having received the Benedictine habit, was chosen Abbot of the monastery. In the year 757 the monks of the Lateran returned to the ancient home of their Order.

By this time, the erstwhile terrible Lombards, having been converted to the Catholic faith, had lost much of their savagery. Their King, Desiderius, even visited Monte Cassino to beg of the Abbot Optatius, who had succeeded Petronax, a colony of monks for the monastery which he wished to found at Leno. His plea was granted, and the monks set out, taking with them as a relic the arm of their holy Founder.

# CHAPTER 10
# PRAYER AND SCHOLASTICA

S t. Benedict was getting old. Every day brought him a little nearer to that heavenly country for which his soul had always yearned. To him death was but the entrance to a larger life, the messenger of eternal freedom, for he who lives for God has Paradise already in his soul.

Since the day when as a young man he had gone forth from his father's house, Benedict's life, like that of St. Paul, had been a dying daily. He rigidly subjugated his body," says Faustus, a monk of Monte Cassino, "by fasting, abstinence, watching, and exposure to cold. We have often seen him during Lent without tunic or hood, clothed in sackcloth, and only twice in the week tasting, rather than eating, a crust of bread." The greater part of his life was spent in prayer, and the walls of that upper room in the tower, which he had made his oratory, might have told strange tales of the heavenly visions vouchsafed to him. It was whispered among the brethren that he came forth from these long communings with God surrounded by a strange, unearthly light, the faint reflection of the radiance which was within.

The night was his favourite time for prayer; its silence had always drawn his soul to God; the starlit sky spoke to him of eternity. The very mountain peaks, soaring into the mysterious darkness, seemed to be feeling for that heaven which was so far and yet so near. It was during the still night hours that he had led the little Placid up the steep hillside to teach him the power of prayer; and it was in the night, when praying at the open window of his oratory, that he saw the most wonderful vision of his life. There was a certain deacon named Servandus, Abbot of a neighbouring monastery, who frequently came to Monte Cassino to visit Benedict, and to speak with him of the things of God. He, too, was a man of prayer, and the two saintly souls would talk for hours together of that heavenly country which their hearts desired.

One night when Servandus was sleeping in the lower room of the tower, St. Benedict, who was in the upper room, arose, and went, as was his wont, to pray at the open window. As he stood lost in contemplation, looking out into the night, the darkness was suddenly cloven by a brilliant ray of light in which it seemed to him that the whole world was made visible to his eyes, and as he continued to gaze steadfastly upon the heavenly radiance, he beheld the soul of Germanus, Bishop of Capua, borne upwards by angels in a globe of fire to heaven.

The Saint called loudly to his friend to come and witness the marvel, but by the time Servandus had reached the window only the few last rays of the light were to be discerned. Benedict, having related to him what he had seen, called the monk Theoprobus and bade him send at once to Capua to ask what had befallen the Bishop. The messenger returned with the news of Germanus' death, which had taken place at the very moment when the Saint had seen the vision.

In the valley below the mountain stood the convent of Piumarola, over which Scholastica, the beloved twin sister of St. Benedict, ruled as Abbess. The convent was under Benedict's direction and followed his Rule, but the intercourse between the Abbess and the Saint seems to have been mostly carried on by letters or through messengers. Only once a year did the brother and sister meet, and this was on the mountain side in a house belonging to the monastery and within its gates.

The time had come round for this yearly conference, and the Saint, accompanied by a few of his disciples, came down to the place of meeting, where Scholastica was already awaiting him. The hours passed quickly as they sat together talking of God and of Eternity, and to Scholastica the day seemed all too short. They supped together, and, as the time drew near when Benedict was wont to return to his monastery, his sister, who seems to have a strange intuition that they would see each other no more on earth, besought him earnestly not to leave her, but to pass the night with her in conversation.

"Do not leave me, I entreat of thee," she begged; "let us remain here until the morning that we may speak together of the heavenly life."

"What dost thou ask of me, my sister?" replied Benedict; "it is impossible for me to pass the night outside of my monastery."

Scholastica made no answer, but, folding her

hands upon the table, she bowed her head in silent prayer.

The night was clear, and not a cloud was to be seen; but as she prayed the sky grew dark; torrents of rain began to fall; the thunder growled; the lightning flashed; a terrible storm arose. Benedict went to the door and looked out, but it was impossible to leave the house in such a tempest.

Scholastica raised her head and looked at him. "May Almighty God have pity on thee, my sister," he said; "what hast thou done?" "My brother," was the answer, "I entreated thee and thou wouldst not hear; I had recourse to my Lord, and He has had compassion on me and has heard my prayer. Go forth now if thou canst; leave me alone and return to thy monastery." There was nothing to be done but to bow to the Will of God. Benedict sat down, therefore, and conversed with Scholastica until her soul was satisfied.

Of what did they speak in that last nocturnal interview? Was it of their childhood's home in Nursia, of their first thoughts of God, of their desire to belong to Him, and of how that desire had been granted? We do not know. But when the morning light broke over the mountain top, and the storm had spent itself, the two Saints parted, Benedict to return to his monastery on the height, Scholastica to her convent in the valley. Nevermore were they destined to speak together on the mountain side. But the parting was not to be for long; within a few weeks they were to meet in that heavenly city which their souls had desired so ardently, and where partings are no more.

A few weeks later, as Benedict stood at the window of his cell praying, he saw the soul of his sister, under the form of a snow-white dove, winging its way to heaven. So greatly did he rejoice in her happiness, that, forgetful of his own sorrow, he poured out his heart in thanksgiving to God. Then, calling together the brethren, and making known to them that Scholastica was dead, he bade them go to Piumarola and take possession of the holy body, that it might rest in the tomb that he had already prepared for himself in the oratory of St. John the Baptist on the mountain top. Thus, as St. Gregory tells us, those who had been one in heart and soul on earth were not separated in death.

The place where Benedict and Scholastica had held their last meeting became hence-forward a place of pilgrimage. A little oratory was built there and dedicated to St. Scholastica. The remains of it are yet to be seen, although in the sixteenth century, having fallen into ruins, it was replaced by a larger church.

The monastery of Piumarola, of which the Saint had been Abbess, was destroyed at the same time as that of Monte Cassino, by the Lombard duke, Zoto of Beneventum. The Lombards, the last barbarian invaders of Italy, were a people partly Arian, partly pagan, and wholly cruel. They owed their conversion to the Catholic faith to their Queen Theodelinda, a woman as noble in nature as she was beautiful in face. On the death of King Anthari, her first husband, the Lombards, realizing the worth of the young widow, determined that she should remain their Queen, and that the man whom she should choose for her second husband should wear the royal crown. Theodelinda married Agilulf, Duke of Turin, a brave soldier who proved himself to be also a capable ruler. A fervent Catholic herself, her influence over her Arian husband was such that he became a staunch adherent of the Church, and through the good offices of St. Gregory the Great, and the entreaties of his wife, made peace with the Emperor Maurice. The son that was born to Theodelinda was publicly baptized by a Catholic prelate, a thing hitherto forbidden by the Lombard laws. In the beautiful basilica of Monza, built by the King and Queen, the famous iron crown of Lombardy, sent to Theodelinda and her husband by the Pope, in recognition of their services to religion, is preserved to the present day.

At the time of the first Lombard invasion, when the monasteries of Monte Cassino and Piumarola were destroyed, the nuns, like many of the monks, fled to Rome, where they were housed and supported by St. Gregory. It was to the prayers, tears, and fastings of these holy women, he declared, that the city owed its deliverance, when besieged by the Lombard army.

Piumarola was not the only Benedictine convent in Italy. Justina, one of the spiritual daughters of St. Scholastica, was Abbess of another religious house near Old Capua, the episcopal city of St. Germanus, whose soul St. Benedict had seen carried to heaven by the angels.

When the monastery of Monte Cassino was again restored, Piumarola was rebuilt under circumstances less strange in the eighth century than they appear to us in the twentieth. Ratchis, King of the Lombards, having resolved to exchange an earthly crown for a heavenly, renounced his kingdom and, presenting himself in Rome before

Pope Zachary, asked to be clothed in the Benedictine habit.

With his own hands the Pope cut off the long
hair worn as a sign of royalty by the Lombard Kings,
gave him the tonsure, and vested him in the tunic
and cowl of a monk. Ratchis retired to the Abbey of
Monte Cassino, where he lived until his death. His
wife Tassia, who with her daughter Ratruda also
desired to embrace the religious life, having rebuilt
the convent of the holy virgin St. Scholastica, took
the veil and spent the rest of her life within its
walls.

In later years the convents of Benedictine nuns
increased almost as rapidly as those of the monks.
When St. Boniface founded the monastery of Fulda
in Germany, having sent to Monte Cassino certain
monks to bring back an exact account of the cus-
toms observed there, he also made enquiries as to
the life of the nuns of Piumarola. Shortly afterwards
he founded a convent for women and invited St.
Lioba, a cousin of his own, to come over from her
English nunnery at Wimborne to take the direction
of it. The convent was built at Bischofsheim, where
St. Lioba the Abbess became as famous for her great
learning as for her holiness.

When St. Lioba left England she was accompanied by St. Walburga, the sister of St. Willibald and
St. Winibald. When the latter founded a double
monastery in his diocese, he made St. Walburga
Abbess of the nuns, while he himself undertook the
government of the monastery.

# CHAPTER II

# BENEDICT'S DEATH

S carce forty days had passed since St. Benedict had seen the soul of St. Scholastica winging its way to heaven, when he announced to his disciples that he also was about to depart out of this world. In spite of his sixty-three years he was apparently hale and strong, with no sign of illness; their judgment, no less than their hearts, would fain have disbelieved his words, had they not known too well his power of foretelling the future.

In order that all might be in readiness, the Saint ordered the tomb of his sister to be opened. Soon after, being seized with a burning fever, he asked his monks to carry him to the oratory of St. John the Baptist, where he received his last Communion. Then, standing erect, supported in the arms of his disciples, he gave up his soul to the God whom he had served so faithfully, in the peace of a perfect confidence.

Around him the watching brethren, spell-bound in the silence of that holy peace, followed in spirit the soul of their glorious Abbot as it went on its heavenward way. It was not a moment for grief or lamentation; the sorrow of their hearts was hushed into a deep thanksgiving.

On the day of St. Benedict's death St. Maurus had a strange vision, seen also at the same time by one of the monks of Monte Cassino. They beheld a path leading up to heaven from the spot where the Saint had died. It shone with a myriad of lights, and at the top stood the figure of a venerable old man shining also with the same strange radiance. "Do you know," he asked them, "who has passed this way?" They answered in the negative. "This is the pathway by which Benedict, the beloved of God, has entered into heaven," he said. So did St. Maurus learn of the death of his beloved Father, and of his glorious entry into eternal life.

The body of the Saint was laid, as he had desired, beside that of his sister in the Chapel of St. John the Baptist, in the double tomb which remained the most precious treasure of the monks of Monte Cassino.

Thus did Benedict fulfil the great mission with which God had entrusted him, and which was not to end with his life. For he had planted a shoot from which was to spring the tree of Christian civilization; his spirit was to survive in the life of his Order. Chosen to be the great missionary of the Faith to the barbarian nations, he was to lead them into the fold of the Church, cultivating their savage hearts as his monks cultivated the waste and desert lands. Throughout the Middle Ages his Order was to be the centre of all that was best in the civilization of the time. To it our own England owes her conversion from paganism, for the first thought of an organized mission to England took shape in the brain of Gregory, the first Benedictine Pope.

Like Benedict, a Roman youth of noble family, Gregory had been made Prefect of the city at the age of thirty-three. An imposing figure, clad in his purple robes of office, he was to be seen daily driving through the streets of Rome in a chariot drawn by four gaily caparisoned horses. The news broke like a thunder-clap on the astounded Romans when it was announced one day that the noble Prefect, laying aside his silken robes for the rough habit of a monk, had given to the poor all his possessions save his ancestral palace on the Coelian hill, which had become the monastery of St. Andrew. The astonishment became greater still when it was known that it was not as Abbot that Gregory was entering the house of his fathers, but as the humblest among the monks. Everybody knows the subsequent story, his walk through the Roman marketplace where slaves were exposed for sale, the golden-haired Saxon lads with their bright faces, and Gregory's sudden resolve to carry the faith of Christ to their pagan country.

He had not only sought and obtained leave from Pope Benedict I. to preach in England, but had already started, when he was suddenly recalled by the Pope at the urgent request of the Romans, who fully realized his worth. Some twelve years later Gregory succeeded Pelagius II. on the throne of St. Peter, being the first son of St. Benedict to wear the Papal tiara. Now at last he was able to carry out his heart's desire; and, calling to his side Augustine, the Abbot of St. Andrew's, he entrusted him with the conversion of England. On Christmas Day, 597, ten thousand Anglo-Saxons bowed their heads to receive Baptism at the hands of St. Augustine and his monks; the great work was begun.

From this seed sprang the conversion of Germany also, for it was from an English Benedictine monastery that Winfrid, an Anglo-Saxon monk, known to history as St. Boniface, set forth to be the Apostle of the German nation. Having visited Pope Gregory II. in Rome and obtained his blessing on the work, Winfrid went to Bavaria, which he found already Christianized. Thuringia, which had the reputation of being also Christian, he found in a sad state, given over to heathenism and idolatry. His attempts to improve matters meeting with but small success, Boniface went on to Friesland, where he found St. Willibrord, another Anglo-Saxon monk, who had been working for years at the conversion of the people.

For three years they laboured together, during which time many thousands were won to the Faith, and many Christians who had fallen away under persecution were brought back to the fold. Monasteries and convents were founded to help on the work, while Boniface, travelling from place to place, continued to preach with tireless energy in other parts of Germany. Created by the Pope Bishop, and later Archbishop, he founded the famous monastery of Fulda, and suffered martyrdom at the hands of the pagans in the year 752.

In the kingdom of the Franks the Rule of St. Benedict had been so universally adopted by the time of Charlemagne, that the great Emperor could scarcely believe it possible that monasticism of any other kind could ever have existed. He was an earnest admirer of the Rule of St. Benedict, and during his reign the Benedictine monasteries spread and flourished throughout his kingdom. The famous Abbey of Cluny, founded in Burgundy in the year 910, became one of the greatest centres of revival and reform in the Middle Ages, while the Abbey of St. Gall, founded by the Saint whose name it bore, fulfilled the same mission in Switzerland.

So did the Order of St. Benedict continue the work of its holy Founder, adding to the conversion and civilization of the Teutonic races the education of the people and the cultivation of art and literature. Wherever the monks went they taught the nobility of labour, changing barren deserts into fruitful fields, draining marshes, converting the outlaw and the thief, preaching the Faith by word and example, and showing to all men the beauty of a life lived for God alone. It was the spirit of St. Benedict that lived in St. Augustine, St. Mellitus, St. Paulinus, St. Bede, and all those holy men of Anglo-Saxon times who won for England her name of the Island of Saints. It was the monks again who, to help their poorer neighbours, built and repaired bridges and roads, doing all that was possible to improve the condition of the people amongst whom they had made their home. Schools were opened, and magnificent libraries were formed by their industry and patience.

At the famous monastery of York the monk Alcuin, one of the most renowned scholars of his time, taught the seven liberal arts with such brilliant results that Charlemagne sent for him to stimulate the revival of letters in his empire; while it was from the Benedictine schools of Paris, Tours, and Lyons that the great French universities sprang into being. The monastery of Bec in Normandy became, under Lanfranc and Anselm, a centre of education second only to Cluny in Burgundy, and shared with that monastery the reputation of being the chief stronghold of learning in France. The seed that developed into our own university of Cambridge was sown in the Benedictine school founded there by the monks of Croyland Abbey.

Nor was it in learning alone that the sons of St. Benedict were the leaders of civilization. The scriptoria, or writing schools, of the Benedictine abbeys were the only book manufactories that existed before the invention of printing. There all the rare manuscripts of antiquity were copied and preserved; the abbeys of Fontanelle, Reims, and Corbie being especially noted for their beautiful work.

It is not only as copyists that the monks have earned the world's gratitude. The greater part of the history of the Middle Ages was written in the cloister; St. Bede, William of Malmesbury, Matthew Paris, and Eadmer of Canterbury were all Benedictine monks. The great abbeys were also the centres of art, science, and of all the humbler crafts that go to make up beauty. The monks of St. Gall and of Monte Cassino were justly famous for their exquisite illuminations and mosaic work; while to the latter monastery is attributed the invention of stained glass. The great St. Dunstan, we are told, was not only noted for his beautiful writing and painting, but was moreover an adept in the carving of wood and bone, moulding in wax, working in gold, brass, iron, and silver. Such were the accomplishments of a Benedictine Abbot in the tenth century, accomplishments which St. Benedict himself had laid down as fitting and suitable for a monk. Most of the great monasteries had their studios and workshops, where architecture, painting, and sculpture, as well as the lesser crafts already mentioned, were taught and practised.

Ecclesiastical architecture was introduced into England by St. Bennet Biscop, a monk of Wearmouth, who had mastered its rules in Rome. The ruins of Croyland Abbey, Tintern, and Fountains in our own country, of Fontevrault and St. Denis in France, not to mention the great cathedrals of Canterbury, Durham, and Gloucester, bear witness to the skill of the monastic architect. Nor in the building of the monasteries was it always the Abbot who directed the work. More often than not it was a humble but gifted monk who was chief architect, while the Abbot wrought under his directions as a simple workman. This was the case with Herluin, founder and first Abbot of the monastery of Bec in Normandy, who, great and noble as he was by birth, carried stones and mortar like the humblest mason.

Many of the monks were artists of no mean order. Mannius, Abbot of Evesham, was renowned as a goldsmith, as well as a musician and painter. The walls of the church of the Abbey of St. Gall, built in the tenth century, were covered with paintings executed by the brethren; while the frescoes of the Abbey Church of St. Savin in Poitou are still the admiration of artists. That the Benedictines made use of their artistic talents in their missions to the heathens, we know through the story of the conversion of the King of the Bulgarians, in the ninth century, effected by means of a picture of the Last Judgment, painted on the walls of his palace by the monk Methodius.

The pictures and the stained-glass windows of the churches were often the only books of the unlearned, who, while they prayed, could meditate on the scenes from the old Testament, or the Life of Our Lord thus presented to their devotion.

The father of ecclesiastical music was St. Gregory the Great, the first Benedictine Pope, who introduced the chant known by his name, still recognized as the most solemn and prayerful of all the forms of psalmody. The very organ itself, originally introduced from Constantinople, owes its development and its perfection to the labours of the monks.

Thus did the Order of St. Benedict, throughout the centuries that followed the death of their holy Founder, work for the world's welfare as well as for its holiness, for beauty as well as for utility. Other religious Orders have arisen as the need for them became manifest, and they have done their work or are doing it. Others may arise in the days to come, for there is scope for all kinds of good work in the world; but the Order of St. Benedict still remains: "It is rooted," as one of its great Abbots has said, "in the clay of the Faith."

www.ingramcontent.com/pod-product-compliance
Lightning Source LLC
Chambersburg PA
CBHW020800130626
46554CB00006B/2281